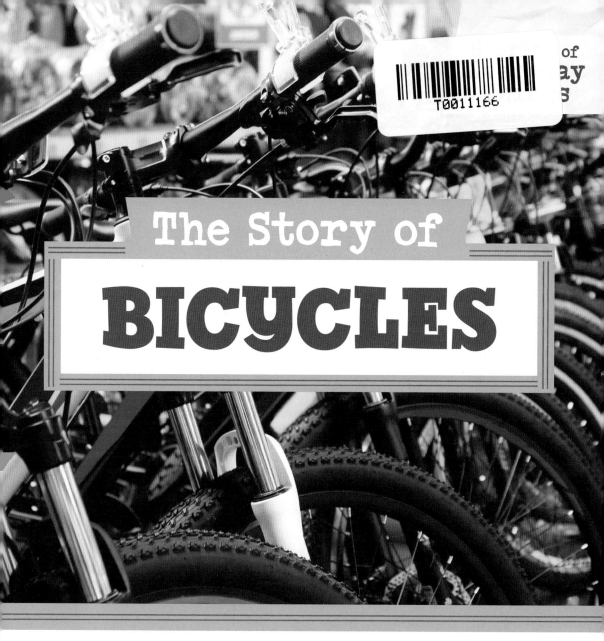

The Story of
BICYCLES

by Mae Respicio

PEBBLE
a capstone imprint

Published by Pebble, an imprint of Capstone
1710 Roe Crest Drive, North Mankato, Minnesota 56003
capstonepub.com

Library of Congress Cataloging-in-Publication Data
is available on the Library of Congress website
ISBN: 9780756577476 (hardcover)
ISBN: 9780756577698 (paperback)
ISBN: 9780756577537 (ebook PDF)

Summary: Learn all about bikes in this fact-filled book.

Editorial Credits
Editor: Christianne Jones; Designer: Jaime Willems;
Media Researcher: Rebekah Hubstenberger; Production
Specialist: Whitney Schaefer

Image Credits
Getty Images: Anadolu Agency/Mehmet Emin
Menguarslan, 22, Hulton Archive, 7, 8, iStock/SergZSV, 12,
Jonathan Knowles, Back Cover, 27, Octavio Passos, 19,
Oli Scarff, 18, Sean Gallup, 16, Three Lions, 11; Library of
Congress: Prints and Photographs Division/National Child
Labor Committee collection, 10; Shutterstock: aerogondo2,
26, Africa Studio, 1, Craig Wactor, 29, Dee Browning, 25,
DODO HAWE, 15, Everett Collection, 9, Monkey Business
Images, 5, 17, Nomad_Soul, 21, 23, s_oleg, Cover

Design Elements
Shutterstock: Luria, Pooretat moonsana

All internet sites appearing in back matter were available
and accurate when this book was sent to press.

Printed and bound in China.   PO 5593

Table of Contents

Words in bold appear in the glossary.

History of Bicycles

They take us places. They help us exercise. They entertain us. What are they? Bicycles! Bicycles are used by all kinds of people. They are everywhere, all over the globe.

Today, there are more than 1 billion bicycles in the world. Denmark has more bikes than cars! But how did bicycles begin?

In 1817, a German man named Karl von Drais invented the horseless carriage. It had two wheels but no pedals. So how did it move? Riders pushed their feet on the ground.

This machine was known by many names. The velocipede. The hobby horse. The running machine. No matter what it was called, it led to what we now think of as the bicycle.

People riding hobby horses

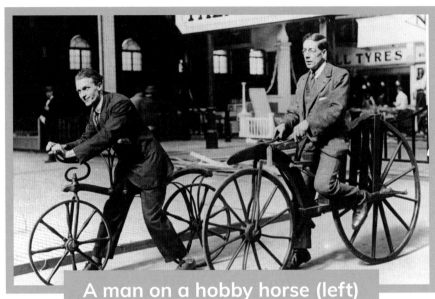

A man on a hobby horse (left) and a boneshaker (right)

In the 1860s, the bicycle changed. Many French inventors tried new things. They added pedals to their models. These were the first machines to be called bicycles. They were also called boneshakers because the ride was so bumpy.

In the 1870s and 1880s, many inventors designed bikes. Eugène Meyer and James Starley gave bikes bigger front wheels. These bikes were called penny-farthings. They were fast and **stable**. People raced them.

William Martin won a New York race riding a penny-farthing in 1891.

A child on a bicycle in Syracuse, New York, in 1910

But riders felt penny-farthings were not safe. Other inventors added safety features. They made the wheels the same size. They gave bicycles chains.

In the 1890s, the bicycle business in the United States took off. Bikes were affordable and easy to fix. This made bicycling very popular.

By 1912, bikes were used for different things. People rode to work. They also rode for fun. Riders were young and old. Bikes were similar to how we know them now.

The son of Scottish inventor John Dunlop rode one of the first bikes to have air in the tires.

Bicycle Basics

A bicycle has basic parts. The frame gives a bike strength. The seat, pedals, handlebars, wheels, chains, and brakes are attached to the frame. Most bikes have gear shifters. Gears can make pedaling easier while going up and down hills.

A gear shift lever attached to the handlebars

What powers a bike? Our energy! A cyclist's feet push the pedals. The pedals are connected by a chain. When a rider pedals, the back wheel turns. The tire uses **friction** to grip the surface and move forward. Handlebars help to steer.

How Bicycles Are Made Today

Around 100 million bicycles are built each year. They are built by workers, craftspeople, and machines around the world. Many bikes are built in Asia. The country that makes the most bikes is China.

Bicycles are **manufactured** through a supply chain. A supply chain is all of the people and ways a product moves from start to finish. The supply chain begins with materials. It ends with the customer.

A bicycle factory in Indonesia

A worker makes steel in a factory.

Every bike begins as raw materials. These can be steel, aluminum, titanium, and carbon fiber. Some parts can be made from rubber, plastic, wood, and leather.

Even recycled materials can be used to make bike parts. Recycled plastic, bamboo, and wood can be used to make bicycle frames.

Bicycle with a bamboo frame

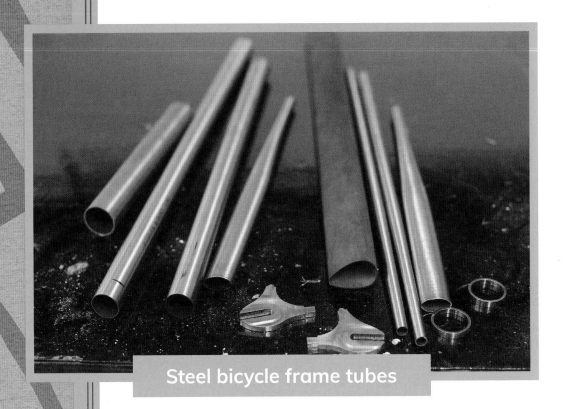

Steel bicycle frame tubes

A bicycle frame and all of its parts are made separately. They are put together in factories by people and machines.

Frames are made from tubes. The tubes are metal and hollow. Machines cut and bend them into the right shapes and lengths.

Workers, or sometimes machines, **weld** the frames together. After a frame is formed, it goes on a conveyor belt. It is painted by a spray gun machine. Then it is dried and baked. Logos are put on last.

Carbon fiber bicycle frame

Then comes the handlebars, brakes, gears, chains, and wheels. Each part has its own manufacturing process. The process uses people and machines.

People install spokes on the wheels. Machines help screw the spokes into the rims. Then a worker inserts an inner tube into the rim. They put the wheel back onto a machine. The machine tightens all the parts. Then a person puts the rubber tire piece over the inner tube. The wheel is complete.

A person attaches spokes to a wheel.

At the end of the process, all the bike parts are checked. Workers make sure the bolts are tight and everything is balanced.

A worker checks the final product.

The finished bike parts are put in a box.

The bike parts are loaded into a box. The bike is not put together yet. It has to get to a store first.

But how does that happen? By **distribution**! The finished parts get delivered to stores all over the world.

How Bicycles Reach Us

You can find bikes at sports stores, bicycle shops, and many other places. Some stores buy bikes from people. They sell them used. Other stores buy bikes from the manufacturer. Manufacturers ship bicycles all over the world. Bikes are expensive to ship because of their shape and size.

When stores buy bikes overseas, the boxes travel by ships to **ports**. When they arrive, trucks pick them up for delivery. Then comes the last stop. The bikes are finally at the store!

Electric bike

Today, there are many kinds of bikes. Road bikes are for paved surfaces. Mountain bikes go on rugged surfaces. Electric bikes have a motor to help cyclists while they are pedaling.

Everywhere, all over the world, people enjoy bikes. They're one of many everyday things used in our everyday lives.

The Penny Plonk

Riding a bike is fun, and there are many games and activities that can make it even more fun! The Penny Plonk is an outdoor bike game. You can play it alone or with friends.

What you need:

- at least five empty containers (like plastic cups or buckets)
- chalk
- pennies (the amount should match the number of containers)
- a timer

What you do:

1. Draw long lines on the sidewalk using chalk. Make them straight or squiggly.

2. Set the empty containers along the lines.

3. Start your timer and get going!

4. As you pass a container on your bike, try to drop (or plonk) in your penny.

5. Time yourself and see how many pennies you can plonk!

GLOSSARY

carriage (KAIR-ij)—a four-wheeled, horse-drawn vehicle to carry people

distribution (dis-truh-BYOO-shuhn)—the way something is delivered

friction (FRIK-shuhn)—the resistance of motion when one object rubs against another object

manufacture (man-yuh-FAK-chur)—when something is made from raw materials using hands or machines

port (PORT)—a harbor where ships dock

stable (STAY-buhl)—not easily moved

weld (WEHLD)—heating pieces of metal so that they melt and stick together

READ MORE

Hill, Christina. *Infographics: Supply Chains.* Ann Arbor, MI: Cherry Lake Publishing, 2023.

Schuette, Sarah L. *Bike Safety.* North Mankato, MN: Capstone, 2020.

Toolen, Avery. *From Metal to Bicycle.* Minneapolis: Jump!, 2022.

INTERNET SITES

10 Cool Things About Bicycles
kids.nationalgeographic.com/history/article/ten-fun-facts-about-bikes

History of Bicycles for Kids
bedtimehistorystories.com/history-of-bicycles-for-kids

Kiddle: Bicycle Facts for Kids
kids.kiddle.co/Bicycle

INDEX

ABOUT THE AUTHOR

Mae Respicio is a nonfiction writer and middle grade author whose novel, *The House That Lou Built*, won an Asian/Pacific American Libraries Association Honor Award and was an NPR Best Book. Mae lives with her family in California and some of her favorite everyday things include books, beaches, and ube ice cream.